To: _____

From: _____

Date: _____

Springtime of Faith

by

Jeanette Lockerbie

MOODY PRESS
CHICAGO

© 1990 by
THE MOODY BIBLE INSTITUTE
OF CHICAGO

ISBN: 0-8024-7696-1

7 9 10 8 6

Printed in the United States of America

Contents

1

THE BEST IS YET TO BE

Bible Reading: Psalm 18:26-30

As for God, his way is perfect (v. 30a).

The phrase "The best is yet to be" was something I grew up with, for, in wartime, my father ended each letter to my mother with the statement "The best is yet to be." Mother never forgot it and often quoted it to us.

Likewise, you and I, while seeking to fulfill God's plan for us, need to look forward rather than backward, or, as a friend of mine puts it, need to be "more interested in the view from the windshield than in the one from the rear-view mirror."

Actually, today's believers can become more optimistic by the day, for each new day brings the coming of our Lord that much nearer.

As a new Christian, converted in my late teens, I heard in the church I attended much of the Lord's second coming. It was an exciting truth. Was I naive in believing it literally? I don't think so. On one occasion I was talking about this subject with great enthusiasm with an older believer. "Oh," she responded, in a resigned voice, "they told me that when I was a young girl."

I still remember my eager response: "Well, doesn't that make it all the *nearer*?"

The Bible does make clear that no man knows the day or the hour when the Son of Man shall come. That is God's secret. Nevertheless, it is our reasonable, our blessed, hope.

I recall that about two years ago, the cry went up in some Christian circles that the Lord Jesus would come in a given month, and a three-day span of that particular month was widely published as *gospel*. We can't know when, but we do know that *the best is yet to be*.

12

Think of a particularly good day in your life, a day that for some reason sticks out in your memory as the best day. This memory, however, may not be all wonderful. There may be an "if only" connected with it. "If only this had not been a part of it," or "if only someone else had been a part of it." It was an imperfect "best day."

That will never be true of God's best days for us. As the Bible tells us, God's ways are perfect—and "perfect" must be a degree higher than "best."

God's timing will be right.

God's purposes for us will be only for our good, for our blessing. We read in Jeremiah 29:11, "For I know the thoughts that I think toward you, saith the Lord, thoughts of peace, and not of evil, to give you a future and a hope."

A future and a hope; more than a hope, a *certainty* that the best is yet to be—just a day at a time!

2

A LOVING HEART, A LISTENING EAR

Bible Reading: Psalm 34:15-18

His ears are open unto their cry (v. 15b).

"She's wonderful," I kept hearing about a certain woman. And it wasn't the "wonderful" we use when we can't think of a better word at the time.

Curious—perhaps even a bit skeptical—I asked a few people who knew this woman, "What do you mean by saying she's wonderful?"

And the answer came:

"She's so interested in other people."

"She gives herself. She brings so much joy into other people's lives."

"She thinks about other people first."

All these are very commendable qualities, but they did not quite explain the warmth, the glow that accompanied the "wonderful." Then one day I got it.

"She *listens*," a harried young mother said of this woman. "I can tell her when things pile up on me and I need someone to talk to. I know she really listens, and I feel so much better."

Increasingly I feel that we're a nation of talkers: few of us want to be bothered listening to someone else. Yet there's a therapy in being able to pour out some of our troubles to the right person.

It may be that one reason there's so little joy around, even in some Christian circles, that we are weighed down with problems and have no one with whom to share them. There's a saying, "A trouble shared is a trouble halved." So it would be good if we were to consider how we can help meet this need in our society.

Of course there's listening and there's listening. Real, honest listening demands one special attribute: *unselfishness*. Although it is not specifically named as a fruit of the Spirit, unselfishness is inherent in kindness and goodness and other fruits of the Spirit.

Sometimes we fail our own families by not listening. This is the agonized cry of today's young people.

My son, Bruce, and I have always done a lot of talking. We still do. But one day when he was about nine or ten, he came into the kitchen where I was working and after a few minutes said, "You're not *listening*, Mother."

Not listening—me? I always listened when a person spoke to me. But that day there was something lacking, something he defined as, "You look like you're listening, Mother. But you're not."

What if God did not patiently listen to us?

God does listen. This is one of the great joys of our Christian faith, that we have personal access to Almighty God—and He does listen. We are assured of an attentive hearing whatever the hour, day or night. And we need no appointment.

Perhaps we need to take a keen look at ourselves as to how available we are to someone who needs a listening ear, a loving heart.

3

LETTING OUR LIGHT SHINE

Bible Reading: James 1:22-27

But be ye doers of the word (v. 22a).

The Bible is clear about all important issues. Two primary points are (1) that we can do nothing to earn our salvation and (2) that God expects that as His blood-bought, heaven-bound children we will be *doers* of the Word.

People will rarely be impressed by what we don't do. I think of a couple, new Christians, who moved into a residence for senior citizens. They had not been there long before their neighbors heard about the wonderful change they had experienced so recently. The comment of one neighbor to

17

whom they had witnessed was, "You're certainly a good advertisement for whatever it is you've got." Then she added, "Not like some religious folks I've met." The couple let the term *religious* go by—it was no time to launch a lecture as to the wide difference between religion and Christianity. They just listened as their neighbor continued. "Mostly," she said, "they've been rather dull, do-nothing folks—like they were making it to heaven by what they *don't do*."

We can assume that the unconverted neighbor was not being truly objective, that she was expressing her own bias. Nevertheless, such an instance can cause us to evaluate our own Christian witness.

Nothing is so likely to produce fruit for Christ's glory, nothing is more convincing to the unsaved, than a peaceful, joy-filled, satisfied believer.

Sometimes it might be good if we were to put ourselves in the position of the person to whom we're trying to witness and ask ourselves, "What would convince *me* of the worth of listening to the gospel and believing it?"

Not that we can be "perfect": only God is perfect. But we can, by our daily lives before others, our kindness and caring for others, make Christianity attractive. I know a woman who was, as far as she could determine, the only believer in the large apartment building where she lived. It was a friendly neighborhood where people knew each other, and it was not uncommon for some to poke fun at my Christian friend, singing in a mocking way, "When the roll is called up yonder, I'll be there." She would smile and continue to be a good neighbor, a doer of the Word. Then one day a young woman came to her, heartbroken because her mother was dying. "Will you come and talk to my mother? She's afraid to die." Not only did this neighbor alleviate the fears of the dying woman by pointing her to Jesus, she also helped in every practical way she could.

Oh, yes. Some of her neighbors still continued to make light of her Christian faith, but others began to seek her out. "If being a Christian is what makes you the kind, thoughtful neighbor you are, tell me

—how can *I* become a Christian?'' they would ask.

Through being a doer of the Word, you—and I, too—can glorify God right where we are.

4

WEEDS AND WEED KILLERS

Bible Reading: Matthew 13:1-7

Some fell among thorns (v. 7a).

I've heard it said by people who know about such things that for every plant there is a corresponding weed. This point was reinforced for me one spring as my first daffodil bloomed, and nearby, as though in competition, a dandelion raised its yellow head.

Weeds must surely be among the greatest problems to the farmer or fruit grower. In similar reference, the Bible speaks of "the little foxes that spoil the vines."

What, then, are some of the weeds in the garden of our lives?

Doubt is a destroyer. It was Satan's earliest tactic. Remember how, twisting God's spoken word, Satan said to Eve, "You will not surely die" (Genesis 3:4, NIV*)? And he is in the same diabolical business today.

Discouragement, the feeling that we just can't do it, even though we know we are in the Lord's will, is another of the devil's traps.

Despondency is one more weed that keeps us feeling down.

Despair and *Defeat* are two more of Satan's negative *D*s: twin emotions that ultimately make us give up on some endeavor for the Lord, even give up on ourselves many times.

Since all of us have at one time or another been victims of doubt, discouragement, despondency, despair, and defeat, it's good to know that there is a powerful, victorious antidote to each of these debilitating emotions.

Trust in God will conquer doubt every time. Personally, I find myself turning many times when I'm in doubt to such verses as:

* *New International Version.*

"God is love" (1 John 4:8).

"He cares for you" (1 Peter 5:7, NIV).

"He knows the way that I take" (Job 23:10, NIV).

"I will instruct you and teach you in the way you should go" (Psalm 32:8, NIV).

"This God is our God for ever and ever; He will be our guide even unto death" (Psalm 48:14).

As believers, when doubts arise, our help is twofold: the Word of God and the indwelling Holy Spirit. The Word of God has the answer to every problem as, a day at a time, we make our journey from earth to heaven. And, since it is an immutable law that two things cannot occupy the same space at the same time, God's Word will oust the weeds that would strangle our growth. In their place the fruit of the Spirit can then grow.

And, think—in time we will even have some fruit to pass on to those around us who need it.

5

WHO WANTS TO BE MEEK?

Bible Reading: Matthew 5:1-5

Blessed are the meek (v. 5a).

In Timothy's day, as in ours, meekness was probably not something in which the average person wished to major. The thinking then, as now, probably was: "What is there for the meek person? Where will it get me?"

If we want to know what meekness can do for a person, look at Moses. Numbers 12:3 tells us that "Moses was very meek, above all the men which were upon the face of the earth."

Moses was criticized. His authority was challenged. But God used him. This gave him a place in God's plan and in history that is an example for all who followed him.

"Blessed are the meek" is the third Beatitude, the introduction to Jesus' Sermon on the Mount.

It's significant that the term *blessed,* which means "happy," is in the present tense. It's to apply *now.*

How is meekness demonstrated in daily living? How can we recognize meekness—or be recognized as a meek person?

There's a serenity about such people, a calmness of spirit. They don't go around making mountains out of molehills. The meek are likely to be the more mature Christians in the church and community. As Matthew Henry in his *Commentary* wrote, "the meek would rather forgive twenty wrongs than avenge one."

Nothing makes Christianity more desirable than its portrayal, in all its simplicity and trust, in the life of someone around us. For example, as a new Christian, much of the language was new and strange to me. But there was a beauty of life among the church members, my new friends. Part of it, I now realize, was their meekness. I didn't know enough to recognize it as such; I could, however, sense the happiness. Later, I would learn their secret, although these many years later I still have a way to go before I would be a model of meekness myself.

Sometimes we sing—it's one of my favorite hymns—"Oh, to be like Thee! blessed Redeemer. . . ." A worthy prayer and hymn, but if you and I are ever to grow even a little bit into the image of the Lord Jesus Christ, we will have to become meek and lowly in spirit, as He is.

A specific demonstration of meekness is depicted for us in Paul's letter to the Galatians (6:1, NIV): "Brothers, if someone is caught in a sin, you who are spiritual should restore him gently."

Then, lest there be a tinge of holier-than-thou spirit, Paul cautions them: "But watch yourself, or you also may be tempted."

There can be no true restoration apart from brotherly love and our admission that we, too, are prone to faults for which we need meek-spirited fellow Christians to help us overcome.

6

THE BEST TIME
OF YOUR LIFE

Bible Reading: Acts 20:32-35

It is more blessed to give than to receive (v. 35b).

What is the best time in life?

Ask any child. He'll tell you. It's "When I grow up so that I can do all the things nobody lets me do now."

My grandmother used to tell us children when we talked in that vein, "You're just wishing your life away, child."

Take the teenager. Surely this is "the best time of life." Yet, though freed from the limitations of childhood, many of us would question that this was the best time of our lives.

What of early adulthood with its sky-is-the-limit possibilities? This age, too, has its special frustrations, not the least of which are the multiplied choices it offers while we may be still lacking the wisdom to make lifetime good choices. Then comes the "life begins at forty" thinking. Generally, however, the fortieth milestone makes no appreciable difference in the person or her way of life.

What of the retirees who've looked forward to the magic sixty-five as surely the best time in life? Some find great fulfillment and contentment; others do not.

It would appear, then, that the "best time" is always some other time than the present. Surely God did not intend that this be so.

The best way I've found to insure a worthwhile day is this: first thing in the morning, honestly praying and turning the day over to the Lord. I don't mean in some pious fashion withdrawing from life and "leaving it to the Lord." Rather, I have in mind squarely facing up to the known realities, as well as the unknowns; asking the

Lord to use me, to lead me in such ways that I can be a blessing to someone else. This giving of oneself makes for an especially good day, even a best day, at times.

The Lord Jesus was not just framing a pretty sentence when He said, "It is more blessed to give than to receive."

Can it be that in our pleasant, comfortable way of life we've got things all turned around? We tend to think of a "best time" as a day when everything came our way: no frustrations or disappointments.

However, the inner joy that makes a day stand out as best needs another ingredient: the fulfillment of having given oneself to meet someone else's needs as well as our own.

Some of the emptiest people I know, the Christians who have little joy in their faces and not much excitement in their daily lives, are the ones who are engrossed in meeting their own needs. All too often at the end of the day they sigh, *Another day—and what has it brought me?*

What's the best time to invest ourselves in other people?

The time is *now*. Yesterday is past; tomorrow is not yet here. But today is with us—all twenty-four hours of it, equal for each of us.

The hymn "Work for the Night Is Coming" offers these good lines:

> Give every flying moment
> Something to keep in store. . . .

That is something we can all do—for the best time in our life.

7

WHO IS MY NEIGHBOR?

Bible Reading: Luke 10:25-29

Thou shalt love the Lord thy God . . .
and thy neighbour as thyself (v. 27).

Many of us grew up with the Ten Commandments. Even though Bible reading may not have had a place in our home, nevertheless the Bible had not been outlawed from the schools. In many instances it was a part of the curriculum. We had to memorize certain portions, which almost surely would have included the Ten Commandments. In both the Old Testament (Leviticus 19:18) and in the gospels, we are exhorted to love God and to love our neighbor.

Loving God is four-dimensional; it isn't a vague, purely emotional love. It is premised on the great doctrinal "Hear, O Israel: The Lord our God is one Lord" (Deuteronomy 6:4).

He is to have first place in our hearts.

He is to have first place in our souls—the worship and adoration part of us—the spiritual realm.

And He is to have first place in our minds—the meditation, thinking, decision-making area.

We are to love Him with all our strength—in the doing of things, in practical expressions of love, in the things that can make a difference in the world around us.

But that is not the end of it, all-encompassing as it may seem.

We come next to the part about loving our neighbor as ourself. Nothing difficult about the first part: it's easy to love my neighbor in a general "Good morning! How are you today?" way. But loving my neighbor as I love myself! I'd have to think about that.

Christian teaching says, "Don't love yourself. That's just haughtiness and pride." So, if the degree of my love for my neighbor is dependent on my love for myself, poor neighbor!

How did the Lord Jesus mean for us to love ourselves? On what basis?

Is it not that we are His workmanship and that in His sight we are worthwhile beings, worthwhile enough for Him to give His life for us? Then surely we are not "nobodies," not worms of the dust.

Many times in the Bible we are assured that God loves us. He created us and then redeemed us with the highest ransom ever paid: the blood of Jesus. In ourselves we are not lovable, but God sees us in Christ. Truly appropriating and internalizing that fact will change our lives. It will give us a healthy, balanced, biblical self-image.

When we begin to love ourselves on this basis we will then see other people as we see ourselves. We will begin to view our neighbors differently. We'll begin to love them, to have the same concern for them that we have for ourselves. And we will begin to be the kind of persons the Lord wants us to be.

It's worth thinking about that I can't be a good neighbor until I love both myself and my neighbor.

8

IT'S ALL RIGHT TO CRY

Bible Reading: Psalm 126

They that sow in tears shall reap in joy (v. 5).

I was visiting in a home where the mother wept as she told me about her unsaved son. The other children were happily following the Lord, while the much-loved youngest, Michael, spurned the gospel.

Later, just as we were about to sit down for lunch, the telephone rang and my hostess excused herself. I can see her yet as she returned to the table: her eyes were streaming but she had a broad smile. Throwing her arms around me, she said, "It's Michael. He accepted the Lord last night. Oh, it's so wonderful I can hardly believe it—after all those years!"

And all those tears, I thought. She had sown in tears; now she was reaping with joy. As we rejoiced together, I was reminded of what I had heard a wise pastor say:

When God sends tears, it's so that
He can follow them up with a rainbow.

Yet many people discount the function of tears. We say to one another, "Don't cry! Please don't cry." This is usually well intentioned, but it does nothing to help. Tear ducts are a part of our humanity, and God gave them to us for a purpose.

Sometimes a child is more perceptive in these matters that the adult. For instance, Cindy came home after playing with her little friend Beth and said to her mother, "Mama, Beth's kitty died, and she was very sad." Then, her little face brightening, she added, "But I helped her."

"How did you do that, dear?" her mother asked.

"I cried with her," the child answered.

The understanding, the insight, of a small child!

The Bible does not cover up tears that are shed. John tells us that our Lord Himself wept at the tomb of Lazarus (John 11:35).

Some of the most inspiring words in all the Bible have to do with tears. Revelation 7, with its description of the glories of heaven, ends with the words "and God shall wipe away all tears from their eyes." I've heard more than one preacher elaborate on that verse with, "Who would not want to have tears, when *God* is going to wipe them all away?"

In our everyday dealings—often with people who hurt—when we can't find the right words of consolation, our tears can speak for us.

It's not so many months ago, when the Lord saw fit to take my wonderful husband home to heaven, that a dear friend, Jane, came one afternoon and said, "Jeanette, I came just to cry with you."

No one could have been more welcome or more comforting.

Never despise the ministry of tears.

37

9

BUT WHO AM I?

Bible Reading: John 1:6-12

To them gave he power to become the sons of God (v. 12b).

Have you noticed that some people appear to find their identity in connection with their occupation? Or, sometimes it's in a relationship: "I'm so and so's sister" (or wife, or grandmother). They seem to have no sense of personal identity or personal worth.

Often it takes a crisis, or a change of circumstances such as retirement, to cause us to stop and do some assessing.

When that moment arrives, two questions are usually uppermost in one's mind:

Where am I going?

What am I going to do?

But underlying each of these questions is the bigger philosophical one: Who am I?

These feelings may not always be expressed even in our thoughts. More often we tend to push them down, thinking, perhaps, that it's unspiritual to ask such a question, that it's not acceptable to God. Yet He is the giver of our power to question, as He is of every other faculty we possess.

At the risk of being considered simplistic, let me share with you my own unalterable belief that God has a plan for my life and that He has a plan for your life, too, even though it may be hard for you to accept if things aren't going according to your own plans.

Everyone, at some point, faces trials. It is then that we have a chance to prove for ourselves what Paul teaches in 2 Corinthians 4:17: "Our light affliction, which is but for a moment, works for us." How well I remember the day I stopped at the word *works*. Who ever heard of trials and troubles working for anybody? But that is what the Bible says. It may be difficult at such a moment to be objective about what has *not* changed: I am the same person, and God has not changed. His Word tells us so in Malachi 3:6, "I am the Lord, I change not."

The true believer in the Lord Jesus Christ need never have any problem or confusion about who she is, for, as we read in John 1:12, "As many as received him, to them gave he power to become the sons [children] of God." This is who you are; this is who I am. No longer need we question, "Who am I?"

And that settled in our minds, we can comfortably proceed to show by life and witness that we are, indeed, the children of God.

10

TAKING A COUNT-YOUR-BLESSINGS BREAK

Bible Reading: Psalm 92:1-5

It is a good thing to give thanks unto the Lord (v. 1a).

How often we come across people to whom being thankful seems to make no sense whatever. Marian is such a woman. Her friends can nearly always count on her to be griping about something. Any suggestion that she should thank God for His blessings is met with, "Who, me? What do *I* have to be thankful for?"

Yet, one of the most forthright statements in the Bible is this: "It is a good thing to give thanks unto the Lord" (Psalm 92:1).

We seem to have an innate sense that expressing gratitude is "a good thing." We see this even in the training of our children, for one of the earliest phrases we labor to get a child to say is *thank you*.

Those of us who have been drilled from infancy to say "thank you" may have to take our "thankful spirit" and look at it once in a while. We all have times when we just do not feel thankful.

A short, crisp sentence in the Bible on the subject is found in 1 Thessalonians 5:18: "In every thing give thanks." We can skip lightly over this verse, or we can internalize it and, a day at a time, put it into practice.

When we give thanks to God for everything that happens to us, we are in fact placing the responsibility for our welfare squarely on God's shoulders. Such an attitude causes us to look for God's hand in our circumstances. How much resistance and possible resentment that forestalls.

Accepting God's will for us—and being thankful—is one of the chief faith hurdles for many Christians. Yet, tremendous good comes when we mature into being happy with His choice, for

He knows, He loves, He cares,
Nothing this truth can dim,
God gives the very best to those
Who leave the choice to Him.

One of the practical benefits of cultivating a thankful spirit is that gratitude and griping cannot coexist. Think of the emotional fringe benefits there. A thankful spirit can often prevent frown lines in one's face, while a prolonged whining spirit almost inevitably reveals itself in one's countenance. Much more severe and potentially long-range is the harm we do to our inner selves in being unthankful.

A well-cultivated thankful spirit is both a preventative and an antidote for anxiety. No wonder we're hearing about increasing numbers of the medical and psychology professions investigating this concept.

We are a worry-ridden, anxiety-prone society, and with good reason, in many instances. But every generation has had cause to be anxious—and the timeless counsel of God is that we "be anxious for nothing, but in everything by prayer and supplication with thanksgiving let [our] requests be made known unto God" (Philippians 4:6, NASB*).

In effect, God is saying, "Don't worry." As a friend of mine puts it, "Worry is the interest we pay on something before it happens—and it may never happen!"

When we have a thankful spirit, we find things to be thankful for, all day long. It's good to give ourselves a count-your-blessings break.

* New American Standard Bible.

44

11

THE SPRINGTIME OF FAITH

Bible Reading: Genesis 8:18-22

While the earth remaineth, seed-time and harvest . . . shall not cease (v. 22).

I am a lover of sweet peas. Their delicate pastels and sweet fragrance do something good for me. One spring day a friend, whose fine blossoms I had openly admired, handed me a tiny packet. "It's your sweet pea seeds," she explained with a smile that added even more to the promise of flowers to come.

Earlier we had discussed the planting procedure, so that very day I followed the direction and planted my seeds. As I did, I thought, *This takes some faith. I've seen some pebbles on the beach that appeared to have more life in them than these tiny withered-up seeds.* But, because I had faith in what I could not see, I watered the seeds and left them in God's good care.

I did one more thing that day. I circled the date on my calendar and noted, "Today I planted sweet-pea seeds." Actually, in that note to myself I was expressing this: "I'm expecting something definite to happen as a result of my seed planting—and I'll be counting the days."

God's promises can be likened to seed, and putting our faith to work is a form of seed planting. In an act as specific as planting a seed in the ground, we can figuratively hide a promise from God's Word in our heart and expect something definite to result. And there's nothing faithless about recording the date on which we demonstrated our faith in this way.

We may never see the process by which God honors our faith, any more than we can observe nature at work in bringing to fruition those seemingly dead seeds we planted in faith. All unknown to us, God works out the miracle that produces the beautiful response to the needs we have expressed in prayer.

And, just as we refrain from digging up the seed to see if it's growing, we exercise patience when we await God's response to our faith planting. Meanwhile, we keep the soil of our soul well watered through the Word and believing prayer.

When the enemy of our souls would come —a day at a time—seeking to demoralize us, to break down our trust in a loving, prayer-answering God, with his diabolical "I told you it wouldn't grow," let us meet his onslaughts as others have done before us. I've heard it said that the indomitable Roland Bingham, cofounder of the Sudan Interior Mission, clung to God's promises, flinging in the enemy's face these words:

> Faith, mighty faith, the promise sees
>   And looks to God alone;
> Laughs at impossibilities
>   And cries, "It shall be done."

It is our responsibility to plant the faith seed. It is God's good pleasure to honor our faith and to bring to fruition the answers to our prayers of faith—a day at a time.

12

GETTING YOUR NAME INTO GOD'S BOOK

Bible Reading: Malachi 3:16-18

And a book of remembrance was written (v. 16b).

Few of us will ever see our name in a *Who's Who*. Nor are we likely to make the *Guinness Book of World Records*—and that will not matter much.

There are two books, however, that your name and mine can be in. One is *The Lamb's Book of Life*. Its pages are reserved for those who have accepted Jesus Christ as Lord and Savior, those who are "washed in the blood of the Lamb."

Entry in the second, *God's Book of Remembrance*, is likewise exclusive. This list records the names of those who

feared (revered) the Lord
thought about His Name (only God can read our thoughts)
spoke often one to another about the Lord.

What might keep us from thinking about the Lord and making Him the subject of our conversation one with another? I can't speak for you, but honesty makes me think of an occasion when my conversation should certainly be about the Lord and His Word, and all too often it isn't. I'm thinking of when we hurry out of church on Sunday morning, eager to get to our car and to a favorite restaurant before it gets too crowded.

Sometimes it's the lack of good models in our early Christian days. I thank God for the Christian, who, when I first knew the Lord, had a habit of quoting Malachi 3:16, by way of a testimony. But for this fact, I might have gone for years not ever knowing that this powerful inspirational verse was in the

Bible. As it was, because the words spoke volumes to me, I memorized it early.

Sometimes it's timidity that prevents us from talking about the Lord. Yet, just by channeling a dead-end conversation (maybe about diets, inflation, or "all the bad news") into talking about the Lord, we can change things. We may halt idle or cruel gossip; we may put a rainbow where only clouds have been as people have reinforced each other's gloom.

When we're talking about the Lord, we have an ally in the Holy Spirit. He will take the things we say and make them real to people who need to hear.

Note that Malachi tells us that they "spoke often"—not just periodically in groups and scheduled classes and as they milled around the Temple after worship. And they spoke "one to another"—neighbor with neighbor, friend with friend. How much we can influence other people as, spontaneously, out of our heart's love for Him, we talk about our Lord. I, for one, would not be sitting writing this material—and rejoicing in the truth of it as I write—if someone had not cared enough and dared enough to change

51

the subject and talk about the Lord Jesus Christ in my hearing. That was going beyond "talking one to another."

Are you rejoicing right now that your name is in the Lamb's Book of Life? That is good—but we don't stop there. We need to make sure that our names are also in God's Book of Remembrance.

13

WHEN YOU FEEL GOD HAS FORSAKEN YOU

Bible Reading: Exodus 3:1-8

I have surely seen . . . I know . . . I am come down to deliver (vv. 7-8a).

Do you sometimes feel that you're off in a lonely desert or some backwater that everybody's forgotten? Have you ever come to the place where you think even God doesn't know where you are—worse, that He doesn't care?

Yes, even God's people have such feelings at times.

We can empathize, then, with Moses in his desert experience. How often must he have looked back longingly to the days when he was somebody in the Egyptian court. We can imagine his gloomy thoughts: *Sheep and more sheep—and nothing better to look forward to!*

Then one day everything changed—and Moses never knew a routine day for the rest of his life.

God had a challenge for Moses, but first the Lord dispelled any idea Moses might have had that He had forgotten His people. God said,

"I have surely seen . . .
"I have heard . . .
"I am come down to deliver them."

And God has never changed in His care for His own.

. He knows where you are. He knows the thoughts of your heart, your longings, your discouragements, your hopes, and your fears.

God has His unique ways of speaking to us today—after all, there was only one burning bush.

One day—it could be today—out of the seeming "nothing ever happens," wherever you are, God will break through the monotony. He will speak to you as only He can. He

54

speaks most often through His Word. A verse will leap off the page and be just for you, just for that time. Or, God may use someone else to convey His message, but you will recognize it as from God to meet your special need.

In my own life I've come to look for and to expect good surprises from the Lord—serendipities, some folk call them.

The Lord uses people who are already busy, generally not those who tend to sit around bemoaning their fate. So it pays to be doing something, and there is no lack of things to do for Him and for others around us.

Far from feeling forsaken, that you have no future, listen to this: "I know the plans I have for you, says the Lord. They are plans for good and not for evil, to give you a future and a hope" (Jeremiah 29:11, TLB*).

With such assurance, why not determine to do something worthwhile today—and see what the Lord has in store for tomorrow—and the next day—and the years ahead?

* The Living Bible.

Such a good expectations attitude is healthy, the finest antidote to gloom and pessimism. Why not try it? Almost certainly you will be aware of God's presence as He assures you that He has seen your circumstances—has heard your plea and knows your present need—and that He is ready to do something about it.

14

FORMULA FOR CHANGE

Bible Reading: 2 Corinthians 3:15-18

We . . . beholding as in a glass the glory of the Lord, are changed (v. 18a).

Grandma Andrews has observed her small granddaughter, Angela, gazing long and often at a portrait in the upstairs hall. The child did this same thing every time she visited, and one day Grandma asked, "Why do you so much like looking at the lady in the picture, dear?"

"Oh, *Grandma*," the seven-year-old answered, "the lady in the picture is so *bee-uti-ful*!" She sighed and added, "And oh, dear, Grandma, I want to be just like her."

Angela didn't spell out, "Maybe—if I keep looking long enough—her beauty will rub off on me." She was too young for such expression. But Angela was on the right track. For it's a fact we do tend to become like that which we admire greatly.

The "looking" as a way to change cannot, however, be a casual glance once in a while. It has to be a consistent, regular pursuit. The clue is given in the phrase "looking as in a glass [mirror]"—with that degree of constancy. How often do we look in a mirror? The Bible teaching is that, if we aspire to be like Jesus, we must major on looking at him through His Word at least as frequently as we look in a mirror.

The change will take time. It will be gradual—after all, it has taken a lot of years for us to become what we presently are in every way. But, if our desire to be like the One we love is genuine, and if we don't give up on ourselves, a day at a time we'll begin to take on some of the lovely characteristics of the Lord Jesus. Some of His beauty and compassion will gradually be reflected in our attitudes and behavior.

We may not notice these changes ourselves but oh, how gratifying when others do. The disciples did not realize that their appearance (or behavior) gave them away. It was the people looking on who saw them and took note "that they had been with Jesus."

It's written of Moses, "He [knew] not that the skin of his face shone." But the people in the camp of Israel knew! Moses had spent time in the presence of God, and even the rebellious Israelites were awed by the change in their leader (Exodus 34:29).

Spending more time with the Lord will cut down on the time we can allot to lesser things that would eventually leave their imprint upon us.

Ultimately, then, the question resolves itself into this: "Into whose image do I want to grow and change?"

That question settled, we can proceed at our own pace toward being transformed into the image of Christ. That is surely God's intent for all His children.

It is never too late to start changing. This very day, we can begin by taking a fresh look at our priorities.

15

A CHALLENGE TO HARMONY

Bible Reading: Romans 12:16-20

As much as lieth in you, live peaceably (v. 18b).

Susan glanced out her kitchen window, and seeing someone coming up the walk she let out a sigh. "Oh no! Not her again," she groaned. That woman!

It didn't take any imagination to interpret Susan's feelings at that moment, or her relationship with the neighbor in question.

To be sure, it does take a good measure of grace to put up with certain people. If we are honest, most of us will admit to such feelings at times. Nevertheless, honesty will cause us to admit that we all have our foibles, our peculiarities, that we, too, can be hard to put up with at times.

We are individuals—made in God's image, to be sure—yet each of us unique.

Although it is God's will that we live in harmony with those around us, many of us have to admit to failing at times to live up to God's standards for our relationships with others. How glad we can be, then, for the loophole phrase "If it be possible."

We might ask ourselves, "What would it take to make it possible for me to live in harmony with everyone whose path crosses mine in the course of a day?"

Speaking for myself, it would mean spending extra time in prayer—prayer for more patience, more tolerance, more understanding; more desire to be a blessing to the people with whom I would act and interact during the day.

Living in harmony with one another also calls for a willingness to listen to each other, without which there can be little fellowship, no matter how much time we might spend together.

"If it be possible," the verse reads. Who, then, is responsible for making possible this desirable peace?

It will take each one of us. I'm so glad that the Lord has not laid upon some and not others the responsibility of living peaceably together. Aren't you?

We have a choice as to how we greet and treat a neighbor who comes to our door. We don't have to react as did Susan and groan, *Oh, not her again!*

It humbles me when I stop to think that someone may be on her knees right now, praying for grace to live peaceably with me.

16

COMMITTING OR CONSIGNING

Bible Reading: Psalm 37:1-6

Commit thy way unto the Lord (v. 5a).

The Scripture for the neighborhood women's Bible study was Psalm 37. A member who had been well up in years when she became a believer always had questions, for the Bible was still a new book to her.

"Will someone please tell me," she asked, "how I can commit my way to the Lord? That seems so vague—so, I don't know how to explain it," she fumbled. "I just don't know what it's saying."

After some thought, one of the group offered to share what the verse said to her. "I used to feel like you do, and for the same reason. I was a new believer. Then the Lord led me to see how I could make it simple: just change 'way' to 'day'—one letter different. Instead of trying to commit my way, I translated it to committing my *day*. I can handle that," she explained.

A wise suggestion? I think we can conclude that it is, since our "way" in the context of verse 5 is the sum of our days. As Annie Johnston Flint has written:

> One day at a time,
>   and the day is His day;
> He hath numbered its hours,
>   though they haste or delay.[1]

A related question might be, "What does *commit* mean, in the practical sense? Sometimes contrasts are effective in clarifying meanings. Take the two words *commit* and *consign,* for example. We commit some things; we consign others. For instance, we consign trash to the garbage can. We just want to get rid of it. On the other hand,

1. Annie Johnson Flint, "One Day at a Time." Reprinted by permission of Evangelical Publishers.

something of value we commit into safe-keeping. We commit (trust) important documents to a safety deposit box. The apostle Paul was dealing with eternal truths when he wrote, "I know whom I have believed, and am persuaded that He is able to keep that which I have committed unto him against that day" (2 Timothy 1:12).

What had Paul committed? His *eternal destiny*. This is the all-time most vital commitment we will ever make. The certainty of our eternal life can be safely committed to Christ alone: "Christ in you, the hope of glory" (Colossians 1:27).

How comforting to know that we can commit both our day and our way to the Lord.

17

HEAVEN:
SOMETHING FOR EVERYBODY

Bible Reading: Revelation 7:13-17

*They shall hunger no more, neither
thirst any more (v. 16a).*

When you let your mind dwell on the
heaven that's awaiting us as believers in our
Lord Jesus Christ, what prospect especially
excites you (in addition to being in His very
presence)?

Pondering this hope one day, it came to
me that quite possibly we view heaven as
providing what earth has deprived us of.
Then, pursuing this thinking, I realized that
for untold millions in our world today,
"heaven" would mean not seeing their chil-

dren starve. For them, "they shall hunger no more" would be the best news they could ever hear. The Lamb (Jesus Himself) shall feed them (v. 17).

And what of the thirsty? It's a fact that we can survive longer without food than without water. Heaven will know no thirst, for the heavenly provision is "living fountains of water": a never-failing supply.

Another blessed prospect is shade from the burning heat of unrelenting sunshine. For many years I lived in Southern California—and what a consolation in the heat of the day to know that sundown will bring needed relief. It's not so in many parts of the world.

One of heaven's prospects that delights me is that I will not be getting lost all the time as I tend to do all too often down here, for Jesus will lead us and be our guide. I won't be looking around helplessly wondering which way to Glory Road (or some other of heaven's addresses).

Without a doubt the most looked-forward-to promise is this: "And God shall wipe away all tears from their eyes." All tears? Yes. Even the tears we shed because a child is smitten with cancer, or tears shed because other loved ones are victims of dread diseases. I'm reminded of the verse in Isaiah 33:24, "And the inhabitant shall not say, I am sick." That is one of the joys and consolations of heaven.

Back to the tears: for whatever reason we weep, who would want to be without tears when God Himself shall wipe them all away?

Because of all the glories that await the Christian, should we not be about our Father's business, assuring by our prayers and our faithful witness that others will be there who might otherwise miss out on heaven and all its joys? That heaven of which we read, "Eye hath not seen, nor ear heard, . . . the things which God hath prepared for them that love him" (2 Corinthians 2:9)—a heaven in which there is something to meet the needs of everybody.

18

THE GREATEST ADVENTURE IN THE WORLD

Bible Reading: Ephesians 4:29-32

And be ye kind one to another (v. 32a).

Some years ago I heard Dr. William McDermont, minister and author, say, "The greatest adventure in the world is being kind."

Inherent in the word *adventure* is the idea of something new and different. So, if you and I aspire to being adventurers, it will involve our finding new and different ways to be kind—and these shouldn't be too hard to find.

Children have an uncanny way of sensing genuine kindness. Take eight-year-old

Jimmy, for example. He and his mother were walking to the grocery store, and along the way they saw a woman working in her front yard. As this woman gave a cheery wave in their direction, Jimmy turned to his mother and said, "She's *so kind* to us kids," and he returned the wave.

The light on Jimmy's face made his mother inquire, "What do you mean, 'she's so kind'?"

"Oh—" Jimmy scratched his head and thought for a second, then answered, "She's just *kind*. She never yells at us kids, even when our ball goes over into her yard. Instead, she calls, *"I'll* get it, boys." Then she tosses it back to us. No griping at us. I guess she likes kids, Mom," he summed up.

It may seem incredible that a Christian has to be reminded of the value of kindness. But apparently we do, for the Bible is careful to spell it out for us: "Be ye kind one to another," our text for today, and, "Love is kind," we are reminded in the "love chapter" (1 Corinthians 13:4, NIV).

If we are going to take the Bible as our standard of conduct, we can't help getting in on this great adventure. And nowhere will this count more than in our own homes, with our children and grandchildren. We can start with little kindnesses and move on to bigger ones. Before we know it, kindness will have become a habit. Not only so, but it can be contagious. One family member observes another showing kindness to the other, and he (or she) is impressed to do likewise. And so it goes: a chain reaction of kindnesses—and the whole family gets in on the great adventure.

Today is the best of all days to begin —right at home.

Wouldn't it be wonderful to be able to eavesdrop one day when your grandson or granddaughter is bragging, "You should meet my grandma. She's the greatest: she's so *kind*." (Then stick around and listen to more of the same.) It can happen when being kind is the greatest adventure in your world.

19

THE LORD OF OUR NOW

Bible Reading: Psalm 46:1-3

A very present help (v. 1b).

Not long after the bombing of Hiroshima, I met a young Japanese woman, Yoshi Taguchi. On that fateful day she had been in class in a mission school that she attended, in Hiroshima. In that school she had been exposed to the Bible, but paid little heed to its teaching. She even laughed at her fellow students who "prayed to their desks," as she interpreted their heads bowed in prayer. Now, her body bleeding from countless glass splinters, she was crawling her way home. One Bible verse came to her mind, and she prayed, "God if you are, like the verse says, a *present* God, help me now."

Our faithful Lord kept His Word. Yoshi was somehow able to crawl her way home. She survived the ordeal. Missionaries helped her to come and study in an American Christian college, and, the last time I met her, she was giving her testimony to the "present God" in a California church. What a joyous reunion we had!

A present God. What if "our help cometh from the Lord" were just past tense or reserved for the future? What would be our hope for today—for all the todays in our lives?

Today—now—was what had concerned my friend Yoshi. Undoubtedly you and I will never find ourselves in the same straits as did she. But each of our todays will bring some problem, some crisis that will drive us to call on the Lord for help. Nor will we ever call in vain, never call once too often for God to hear and heed our plea. For He has promised to be with us always (Matthew 28:20)—all the days. And each day as it comes will be "today."

Today—every day—brings its own opportunities and responsibilities. When its

73

hours have wound down and become yesterday, how satisfied will we be with how we
spent them? Like Frances Havergal, we can
pray each morning,

Take my moments and my days;
Let them flow in ceaseless praise.

What better way to make Christ Lord of
our *now?*

20

ACKNOWLEDGING OUR ASSETS

Bible Reading: Psalm 92:12-15

They shall still bring forth fruit in old age (v. 14a).

In her daily Bible reading, Alice had come to Psalm 92 and had paused at the reassuring promise "The righteous shall flourish . . . " (v. 12).

"I can say 'Amen' to that," she said to herself, and added a fervent "Praise God."

Throughout the day her mind dwelt on some of the ways in which she herself was flourishing. The following day a fellow church member voiced the very opposite feelings as they sat over a cup of coffee together. "What do you and I have left?" was the theme of her little pity party. However, she brightened enough to say wistfully, "We must still be of *some* good in the world, I suppose."

It's conceivable that most of us have temporary spells of feeling we have outlived our usefulness, but how much better to dwell on God's special goodness in allowing us to live a long life. We might well "compare it to the alternative," as some do facetiously.

What are some of our most valuable assets gained through the long years?

Wisdom. Nobody is born wise, and some people seem to acquire more wisdom than others. Nevertheless, the mature years generally bring with them a fair measure of wisdom. That is something we can profitably share with younger people.

Experience. Just the fact of having lived a long time has taught us many things. Oh, the cynic may gripe, "I haven't had sixty years' experience. I've had one year's experience sixty times over." But why take our cue from the cynic?

Sound judgment. A degree of ability in good decision making is the product of both wisdom and experience. As Dr. Ralph L. Byron, noted Christian surgeon, once said to me, "Good judgment is developed through poor judgment." Obviously, that is so by reason of the fact that we have to live with the consequences of our decisions—and learn thereby.

Tolerance. Little things do not frustrate us as they once did. We have more patience with the foibles of others and the trials life sends our way. We are less easily provoked.

Increased faith. We can stand on our mountain peak of faith and look back over "all the way the Lord has led us." We recall having stood upon His promises and found ourselves on firm ground. And we have His continuing promises for today, tomorrow, and always.

And isn't it a comforting thought that inflation can never touch or adversely affect our God-given assets?

21

HELP FOR THE "I'M NOBODY" BLUES

Bible Reading: John 15:12-17

I have chosen you (v. 16b).

The desire to be wanted and chosen is something we never quite outgrow. It's as important for the retirees as for the child entering kindergarten.

I was grown up before I learned of the Bible's comforting assurance along this line, for people of all ages. Advised by the Christian who led me to Christ to read my Bible first thing every morning, I was nevertheless totally ignorant of where to begin. I just opened the Bible "at random," and I can see it yet! As though written that very moment, and just for me, the words stood out: "Ye have not chosen me, but I have chosen you" (John 15:16).

"That's *true*," I said aloud. "That's really true, God": my very first conversation with the personal God I was just beginning to know.

Chosen, and this was the Lord Jesus Christ Himself telling me He had chosen me. What a way to begin this new life—with a message as direct and personal as a telegram!

Whether new convert or older member of God's family through faith in Christ, it's a great feeling to realize that He chose us, that we are special to Him. Nothing can cure the "I'm nobody" blues like dwelling on John 15:16. In the course of a day some insensitive person may say or do something that could shake our self-confidence, make us feel worthless. But God's estimate of us never changes. He does not choose us just to later drop us. We are valuable in His sight.

In our youth-oriented society where in all too many instances we older people are relegated to lesser roles, how good it is to keep in mind that the Lord has something special for us to do. He chose us *for* something: "to bring forth fruit"—and there is no "sixty-five" clause attached!

Then, since God is always fair and just, He will require from each of us fruit from the particular ability seed He has planted in us—not oranges from apple seeds or figs from a grape seed. This being so, we can't judge one another as to our fruit-bearing for God: He is the judge of that.

As one of God's chosen ones, we can lift up our head, nurture our special ability seed —and one of these days hear His "well done."

Far from being a nobody, we can rejoice in being one of God's somebodies.

22

BETTER LATE THAN NEVER

Bible Reading: Matthew 20:1-16

I will give unto this last, even as unto thee (v. 14b).

In my travels in Asian countries I've frequently come across typical Bible scenes. For instance, one day when I was visiting my missionary daughter in Bangladesh, I heard her ask someone why he was just standing around. His reply: "No man hired me."

Those who remember the days of the Great Depression can recall the long lines of people waiting, hoping—praying, perhaps—for a job, for someone to hire them. Some may have been hired by the day, some for just a few hours. Some may have gone to work late in the day. But better late than never.

I love that great "better late than never" story that the Lord Jesus told in our reading for today. It's the tale of an employer and his hired men: the "regulars," who showed up at starting time, and the "extras," hired later in the day.

Quitting time came and the workers lined up for their wages, as was the custom of the day. And behold! Those who started late in the day received exactly the same as the "nine-to-five" workmen!

Lest you might be rationalizing, *That doesn't seem fair,* think it over. Did the employer's gesture in paying the part-timers the same amount he paid those who had labored all day take one penny out of the latter's pocket? Had they not contracted to work for a certain sum, which was duly paid them? The part-timers likewise were told what they could expect: "whatsoever is right" (v. 7).

Right in whose eyes? Does not the owner-employer have the last word as to recompensing his employees?

Oh, but there's infinitely more in this parable than a dissertation on the rights of employees. Note the opening verse: "For the kingdom of Heaven is like unto. . . ." What have we been told that a parable is? A dictionary defines it as "a figure of speech," but I have always heard a parable referred to as "an earthly story with a heavenly meaning." I see this "story" as a picture of the person who is on in years, who has perhaps heard the story, but neglected to apply it to herself and thus assure what "the end of the day" would bring for her.

True, it is better late than never. But why wait?

"Behold, now is the accepted time; behold, now is the day of salvation," the Scriptures tell us (2 Corinthians 6:2). And no matter how old we may be, the Lord will welcome us. It will always be better late than never, and even the latest comers will receive whatever is right.

23

THE DISCIPLINE
AND REWARDS OF DELAY

Bible Reading: James 1:1-4

Let patience have her perfect work (v. 4a).

"Some days really try my patience."

How often we hear this complaint, usually with the volume increasing for emphasis.

But can days affect us? Is it not rather the circumstances in which we find ourselves on a given day?

Do the years foster patience in us, or are we who are older just as prone to impatience? And how do we "let patience have her perfect work," as James exhorts us?

Personally, I'm a toe tapper when faced with a delay, and I've been known to flip-

pantly declare, "I've no background for waiting," or (irreverently), "I've never waited
patiently for God or man."

But we're never too old to learn.

Recently, meeting a few friends for
lunch, I arrived at the restaurant on time, to
find none of the others there. Minutes went
by, and I admit my thoughts were pretty negative: *Why couldn't they . . . how can they be
so indifferent to time*—and other self-righ-
teous musing occupied my mind. Fortunate-
ly, my conscience came to my aid, showing
me I was being totally childish and condem-
natory in my attitude.

Not that I would advocate a chronic
lack of punctuality on anyone's part. Rather,
we need to be sensitive to the cause(s) of the
delay. Surely this is one means of "letting
patience have her perfect work."

A great lesson the Lord taught me that
day at the restaurant was this: I had a choice
as to how I reacted to other people's behavior. I could greet my friends with, "So you
finally made it! I've been waiting and *waiting*," and so on. Or, I could step to meet
them with a smile and "Here you are! What
a good time we'll have."

We did have a most enjoyable time—and I gained a notch on the patience ladder, with the good feeling that engenders.

Where would any of us be, I wonder, if it were not for God's infinite patience with us?

How long did He wait while we went our way, neglecting His "Come unto Me"?

24

GOD NEEDS
NO ANSWERING SERVICE

Bible Reading: Jeremiah 33:1-3

Call unto me, and I will answer thee (v. 3a).

Alice's disgust was evident as she turned from the telephone. "Same old thing," she griped to her sister, then mimicked the "You-have-just-reached-the-home-of" greeting she had heard, closing with the exclamation, "I get *so tired* of these answering machines: they dehumanize people."

"Oh, it's not that bad, Alice," her sister, Marian, responded, "they do serve a purpose, and we have to move with the times."

Whatever our reaction to the automatic telephone, it's here to stay, because, as Marian wisely commented, it does serve a purpose. Even the most dedicated family member, neighbor, or friend cannot always be on hand to respond to our phone call.

How satisfying then, to have the assurance that God is always there, that He needs no answering service.

"Call on me and I will answer," His Word promises. No maybes, no stipulations: rather, a firm "I *will* answer."

Why might Alice (and you and I) feel somewhat put out that our call is not answered by the person whom we're calling?

Of course it will depend on the purpose of our call.

When the matter needs an answer, the result will be delay. It will necessitate a second call.

If the purpose of our call was to relay some good news, we will conceivably feel disappointed that the person was not there to share it with—a machine has no emotions.

If we've made the call because we are in need of an understanding listener, we may feel really let down when the answering machine is the substitute—a machine has no understanding.

All the more, then, can we rejoice in knowing that we will never call heaven in vain.

Not only is God always *there,* He is also always *awake,* whatever the hour of the day or night we call on Him.

That reminds me of how Elijah mocked the prophets of Baal about *their* God, when they received no answer from Baal.

"Cry aloud," Elijah mocked, "for . . . peradventure he [Baal] sleepeth and must be awakened" (1 Kings 18:27).

Our God is an ever present, ever watchful, caring God.

When the nights are long and we may be unable to sleep, it will never be too late for God to hear us and to answer as only He can, in the way that is best for each one of us.

God needs no answering service because He is *God.* And, as His blood-bought children, we have a direct line to Him twenty-four hours a day, every day of the week and year.

25

NOTHING TO REJOICE IN?

Bible Reading: Habakkuk 3:17-19

Yet I will rejoice in the Lord (v. 18a).

It's not always easy to rejoice. I have to confess I'm not like the person who wrote, "I feel like singing all the time."

Yet the Bible has much to say to us about rejoicing. Even so, I fear that all too often we tend to excuse ourselves with rationalizations:

"If you knew my home situation!"

"With my health problems, how can *I* rejoice?"

"What do I have to rejoice about—with a fixed income and inflation eating it up?"

These and other justifiable reasons are understandable. Nevertheless the word comes in every generation: "Rejoice ever-more" (1 Thessalonians 5:16). *Evermore!* Paul strengthens this directive with "Rejoice in the Lord always" (Philippians 4:4, NKJV*), regardless of anything and every-thing. It is when we do rejoice in the face of trial and tragedy that God is glorified.

What if Paul and Silas had sat around in that Roman prison griping, maybe railing at God for what had happened to them? What if they had been sulking instead of singing? Would we have the Philippian jailer convert as an example of how to be saved? I once heard a preacher admit, "If I had been in that jail, Paul would have been singing a *solo*."

What, then, is the key to rejoicing ever-more, under all circumstances? Rejoicing *in the Lord.*

Habakkuk sets a great example for us. Against all odds, natural disasters having robbed him of his crops in the fields; his fruit, meat, milk, oil, hides, and wool—prac-tically everything that sustained his physical being—gone, Habakkuk vowed, "Yet I will

*New King James Version.

rejoice in the Lord, I will joy in the God of my salvation."

Such a decision to put his complete trust in the Lord was a distinct act of the will. "I will rejoice . . ."

We never do anything until we will to do it.

We might ask, "What benefit is there for me in rejoicing?" Plenty, we will find. Number one, it makes us feel better inside. Second, it gives credibility to our profession of Christ. People looking on can sense that we are "for real," knowing that in the same circumstances they would probably be doing everything but rejoicing.

A good question to ask ourselves might be, *If I grumble instead of rejoicing, how does my life differ from my unsaved neighbor's?*

There will never come a time when we cannot—if we *will* to—rejoice in the God of our salvation.

26

OUR TICKET TO HEAVEN

Bible Reading: 1 John 4:7-11
God is love (v. 8b).

Can you recall from your earlier days when your church or Sunday school had a contest—and a prize—for memory work?

If you were like me you chose short verses. That way you could memorize more verses. "God is love" was sure to be one most of us learned.

God is love: I memorized it—with its reference, for that counted, too—long before I gave any thought to its meaning in my life.

Let us really think about it.

God *is* love: present tense. Not just yesterday and the day before, when we may have had a particular need for the assurance that God loves us. No. There's no time element to it. It is a yesterday, today, and forever love.

God's love for us cannot be reckoned by our human love one for the other. In spite of our intent, we can and do fail each other at times.

In His love for us, the Lord Jesus Christ is God's love in action. In His life and in His death for us, He is God's love incarnate, in the flesh, and His love never fails us.

Believing that Jesus Christ is the Son of God and the Savior of the world will not, in itself, save us and take us to heaven. That is simply intellectual belief, head belief, if you like.

Accepting Him as our own personal Savior: that comes with a guarantee. As we read in Romans 10:9, "If thou shalt confess with thy mouth the Lord Jesus, and shalt believe in thine heart that God hath raised him from the dead, thou shalt be saved."

Believing and accepting. This combination, by God's grace, is our ticket to heaven.

The question we must ask ourselves, then, if we would make sure of heaven, is this: *Am I wholly trusting, as my only hope of heaven, in the Son of God who loved me and gave Himself for me?*

When we can honestly answer yes, we have our ticket to heaven.

27

THREE HUNDRED SIXTY-SIX FEARS

Bible Reading: Isaiah 41:10-14

Fear thou not; for I am with thee (v. 10a).

Jane and her neighbor, Sharon, had met for their weekly Bible study. Enjoying a cup of coffee prior to getting down to study, Jane was expressing some of her fears concerning their neighborhood. She is not alone in being fearful at times.

The experts tell us that we're all born with two fears: the fear of loud noises and the fear of falling. Are you mentally counting all the things that cause you to fear?

Many times I hear someone say, "I know the Bible tells me to 'fear not,' but how do I, how can I, 'fear not'?" Then the person goes on to enumerate a whole array of fear-producing realities.

Everybody has fears. A few years ago a top scientist admitted, "I'm afraid, and all the aware men I know live with fears."

Fear has·become a sickness of our times. And with good reason. "Nobody is safe," we hear at least once a day. And for one of us to say, "Don't be afraid," would be a mockery. But God can say it! And He does.

Someone has compiled a list of the forms of "fear not" in the Bible. The total is 366—one for each day in the year, and an extra for leap year!

Not all fears should be got rid of, however. Some are warning signals. They are useful. They alert us to take sensible action. Smoke warns of fire. Pain is a "friendly fear"; it's the body's way of signaling, "See your doctor."

It's the fear that comes from daily living —from newspapers, radio, and television with their graphic accounts of horrible happenings; fears that surround us and we can't do anything about them—it's for such fears our loving Lord has given us His promises, His "fear nots."

The disciples showed fear when threatened by the storm-tossed Sea of Galilee. We might wonder at that. Were they not seasoned fishermen? And had they not been long enough with Jesus to trust Him and not be afraid?

The disciples were just like us. In the storm they needed His "Peace be still," His "Fear not, for I am with you."

None of us can live with moment-by-moment fear.

A verse that has come to my aid many times when I've been fearful is "What time I am afraid, I will trust in thee" (Psalm 56:3).

And that is just one of the 366 "fear nots" that can calm us as we put our trust in the Christ of Galilee.

28

IN THE SCHOOL
OF SUFFERING

Bible Reading: Philippians 1:27-30

For unto you it is given . . .to suffer for his sake (v. 29).

How many of us would voluntarily enroll in an advertised School of Suffering? I'm sure I wouldn't.

Yet the Bible calls suffering a gift: "Unto you it is given," Paul tells us, "not only to believe on him, but also to suffer" (v. 29).

Enrolled in this school, we can be assured that we have the master teacher. God is likewise the master designer: He knows how best to perfect that which He has created. God is not toying with ceramics. He is molding us for eternity. And it's not always a pleasant experience. Often we would prefer not to learn, not to be reshaped.

But—and it will take a thousand eternities to fathom this truth—God's divine alchemy produces peace out of pain, sweetness out of sorrow, and beauty from ashes. Who can dispute this? The serenity on the face of a chronic sufferer? The sweet contentment of a poverty-ridden older Christian when the very opposite would be more understandable? In my early days as a believer, one of the greatest sources of inspiration to me and to my fellow new converts was an elderly Scottish woman we called Mother Young. She had little of what the world would consider cause for contentment. Her favorite hymn, which I learned from frequent hearing, was "I Have Christ, What Want I More?"

She sang, not with a spirit of resignation but of deep joy. The radiance in her face was a sight to behold. For, like Amy Carmichael, my friend had learned the secret that *in acceptance lies peace.* Even when her own family mocked her faith.

Whatever trials come our way—and they will, as God works out His will in our

100

lives—we can be patient while in God's school of suffering, for one day we will graduate into His very presence.

Suffering may be physical, emotional, or a combination of the two. And it's as the Lord permits us to go through whatever the trial that we learn for ourselves that He knows, He loves, He cares. Not until then are we really able to enter into the feelings of a fellow sufferer and share with her what Christ can do for her at such a time.

It will always be true for those who love the Lord and strive to live for Him that "weeping may endure for a night, but joy cometh in the morning" (Psalm 30:5).

29

JUST A DAY AT A TIME

Bible Reading: Deuteronomy 33:25-27

As thy days, so shall thy strength be (v. 25b).

Just eight words. But was there ever a more comforting promise?

A Christian friend of mine—a surgeon—was visiting one of his patients. Wearily she looked up at him and asked, "How long must I lie here, doctor? How long will I be in this hospital?"

"Just a day at a time," the kindly doctor answered, and repeated, "Just one day at a time." Then he added, "And as thy days, so shall thy strength be."

I'm reminded of the old hymn, "Lord, for Tomorrow and Its Needs I Do Not Pray."[1] The last verse sums up the thought:

So for tomorrow and its needs
   I do not pray;
But keep me, guide me, hold me, Lord—
   Just for today.

We live by the day.

Yesterday is past; tomorrow is the future with its unknowns.

Today is ours.

We will never have to meet our today alone, never be left to cope with its toil or trial on our own.

With the coming of each new day comes the promise of strength from above. Strength for what?

God's promise encompasses whatever each "today" brings: joy and happiness, or sorrow and heartbreak. Personally I am claiming and clinging to God's promise of strength for each day. For, even while I'm

1. *Sankey's Sacred Songs and Solos,* no. 638. Used with permission of Marshall, Morgan and Scott, Ltd., London.

writing these words, I'm grieving and hurting at the loss of my beloved husband, whom God saw fit to call unto Himself. No, I take back that word *loss*—for my husband is not lost. I know where he is. He is safe with the Lord Jesus, whom He loved and served faithfully.

No matter what the day brings, we can count on God's faithfulness. He *will* keep His Word. He *will* provide strength for whatever He calls us to go through—one day at a time.

30

COPING WITH NIGHT FEARS

Bible Reading: Psalm 4

I will both lay me down in peace, and sleep (v. 8a).

No one will question that we are living in evil days. One of the dread signs is a prevailing fear, especially on the part of the elderly and those who live alone. And seemingly even avowed Christians are among those who are obsessed with such well-founded fears.

Are there, then, no remedies (apart from the locks and bolts and other security devices that are making the manufacturers rich)?

Oh, yes! The Scriptures abound in reassurances for the fearful, and we would do well, for our own peace of mind, to heed them.

In a group Bible study in which I'm involved the topic of night fears surfaced—and what to do with them. It was interesting and enlightening to listen to the ideas expressed. Said one member of the group who admitted to having suffered from such fears: "Living alone as I do, I used to dread the night hours. But now, when I arrive home in the evening, I just lock my doors, look up, and say, 'I'm home, Lord.' Then I leave myself in His care."

Another woman explained how she dealt with her night hour fears: "I wear a hearing aid all day," she told us, "and when I'm ready for bed I just take it out—and I don't hear a thing until I put it back in, in the morning. I've learned to trust my Lord to take care of me."

Those two women, and others who admitted to being afraid when alone at night, and who shared how they had learned to cope with such fears, have much in common with the psalmist David. For he it is who, again and again, gives us the secret of dealing with fears. From his lifelong experiences as shepherd boy on the Bethlehem hills, as soldier, and as king—all occupations at times fraught with danger—David wrote the most comforting, heartening words ever penned, the incomparable Twenty-third Psalm with its "I will fear no evil, for thou art with me." And if these strong promises are not enough to quell our fears, the psalmist further wrote for our comfort and assurance the words "The Lord shall preserve thee from all evil. . . . The Lord shall preserve thy going out and thy coming in" (Psalm 121:7-8a).

When we go out, when we come in, and while we are asleep, as God's blood-bought children we have His protection. Why, then, should we be among the fearful?

31

SAYING YES TO LIFE

Bible Reading: Jeremiah 29:11-13 (NIV)

For I know the plans I have for you (v. 11a).

With a flip of the calendar the day arrives: for better or for worse we have reached retirement age.

How we accept and deal with the change that the not-so-magic "sixty-five" brings is not, generally, determined when we actually reach that milestone. Rather, we are programming ourselves, consciously or unconsciously, for months or even years before we are faced with the inevitable circumstance.

Some people are quite outspoken as to their views of retirement. For instance, I was speaking to a group of women school teachers on the topic of "being the kind of teacher you really want to be." For starters, I suggested that they might share their ideas on the subject with each other—and with me. Without hesitation one spoke up. "The kind of teacher *I* would really like to be," she said, "is a *retired* teacher," and we all had a good laugh. But this teacher meant it. She was not being facetious, was not laughing.

As in every area of life, attitude is the key to action and reaction. All things being equal, a positive attitude toward retirement can mean that we retire not just from but to something.

We're cashing in on the "future and a hope" that the Lord has planned for us.

A few days ago I received an upbeat letter from a couple, both longtime friends of mine. It read in part, "The nine-to-five chapter of our lives is closed, and we can hardly wait for the next adventure."

There is a couple whose future stretches before them with purpose and challenge. Not waiting to be acted upon, they are, themselves, the activators.

Unquestionably, retiring is a crisis, and any crisis normally brings out the best and the worst in us.

All too often, in a sort of protest, the retiree resorts to doing nothing.

Some appear to feel that even God has given up on them; that He has no further work for them to do; that, in fact, they have no tomorrow.

By contrast, a healthy attitude sees retirement age as just a pause on the landing of life, to catch one's breath before tackling the next flight. Such thinking leads to good decision-making; it's "saying *yes* to life" and moving on into the future and the hope that the Lord has promised to each one of us who love, trust, and follow Him.

32

THAT UNRECOGNIZED TALENT

Bible Reading: Romans 12:6-8

*We have different gifts, according to
the grace given us (v. 6a, NIV).*

With a shrug of her shoulders, Anne
quipped, "I must have been behind the door
when the talents were given out."

Perhaps we would all like to disclaim
our God-given abilities at times, for with
ability comes responsibility, according to the
parable Jesus told in Matthew 25:14-30.

It may take another Christian to pin-
point for us a particular talent we have. For
instance, in the course of speaking at a meeting, I started, "I'm a one-talent person," by
way of encouraging my hearers to use what-

ever talent(s) they had. Well, the meeting was scarcely over when a young woman dashed up to me and said, "That's not true what you said tonight." *Goodness me,* I said to myself, *what lie did I tell?* Then she proceeded to enlighten me. "I know about your writing and other things you do, but the best part is that you're good at sitting by the fire and being a friend."

It's evident, then, that we can be using a talent even when we do not recognize that we possess it. How encouraged I felt that evening, but not only so, I've tried with the Holy Spirit's help to sense when "just sitting by the fire and being a friend" was what God required of me.

We might spend a profitable hour with a few friends just helping one another recognize some of the areas of special ability each one of us has been given. By such simple means we can enlighten and encourage one another. This is no time for excuses such as, "I can't do . . . this or that." Rather, it can be a fruitful time for uncovering our areas of ability.

Perhaps we wish we could have had some choice as to which gift or ability would be ours. Maybe we would gladly trade ours off for something that has more appeal for us. But our all-wise God has apportioned His gifts as He wills, and one day He will require from each of us an accounting of our use of those gifts.

Let me underscore a fact that applies equally whatever our use of our God-given abilities: it will involve the giving of our time. Napoleon is reputed to have said, "Ask me for anything but my time." I'm afraid I may be guilty of such feelings myself. I tend to guard my time for what *I* want to be doing.

If you and I really want to be used by our Lord, it will pay us to ferret out what our particular ability is, then get busy putting it to use.

A good question to ask ourselves is this: *If* I *don't do this today, who will?*

33

HOW TO BE AN ENCOURAGER

Bible Reading: 1 Samuel 30:1-6

David encouraged himself in the Lord his God (v. 6b)

One of Satan's sharpest tools is discouragement. If he can so move in our lives that we are overcome by such feelings, he will have won a victory.

Think, then, of King David, that "man after God's own heart." It would seem that every possible evil had befallen him: his city in ruins, his wives and family taken captive. To make it worse, his own men, in their grief and despair over their own losses, threatened to stone him to death. Surely no man ever had more cause to become discouraged.

But even in such dire extremity, David knew where to turn. As our text tells us, he "encouraged himself in the Lord."

Few, if any of us, will ever have such cause to be discouraged. Nevertheless, in our own setting and circumstances, we can at times empathize with this man of God as we, too, face dire situations.

Where do we go for solace and encouragement?

As believers, we should be able to go to one another, and indeed there are some among God's children who particularly seem to have the gift of being encouragers.

What would prevent anyone from wanting to be such a person?

It could be that he or she had been brought up by parents to whom it didn't seem important to encourage their children. What an opportunity and privilege then, for older people—grandparents or other adults who have much to do with the children in the family—to assume the role of the encourager whenever the opportunity affords itself. Of course this must be undertaken in a sensitive manner with not even a suggestion hat the parent(s) might conceivably be failing in this regard.

As for ourselves, when we feel discouraged and in need of some real encouragement, what better step can we take than to emulate David. Like him, we too can encourage ourselves in the Lord our God.

How to do this? you may be asking.

Without a doubt, whatever problem might be troubling you at this very moment is not new or yours alone, for we read in 1 Corinthians 10:13:

> There hath no temptation taken you but such as is common to man: but God is faithful, who will not suffer you to be tempted above that ye are able; but will with the temptation also make a way of escape, that ye may be able to bear it.

Having tested this promise and found it to be true, you can then confidently encourage someone around you who likewise is in need of such assurance. There will always be a need for the encourager. In fact, I have heard it said that encouragement is the oxygen of the soul.

34

DOES JESUS CARE?

Bible Reading: 1 Peter 5:7-11

Casting all your care upon Him, for He cares for you (v. 7, NKJV).

Over the radio came the haunting strains of the hymn "Does Jesus Care?" As the organist played on, to Martha's mind came the words,

> Does Jesus care when I've said goodbye
> To the dearest on earth to me?

Following the recent death of her husband of over thirty years, Martha badly needed an answer to that poignant question.

Was it coincidence, then, that right at that moment the telephone rang? It was a neighbor, Susan, inviting Martha over for a cup of tea.

"It'll do you good, Martha, to get out of the house for a little while. Anyway," she coaxed, "I've just baked a batch of your favorite muffins."

Martha didn't feel one bit like being done good to; she would have preferred to be left alone with her grief. But she somehow roused herself, combed her hair, and made her way over to the neighbor's. There, in an atmosphere of understanding, she was able to talk about the anguish she was feeling, the despair, the fears that gripped her in her loneliness.

Does Jesus care?

We would not be honest if we didn't admit that there have been times when we have questioned whether God really does care for us. But God in His heaven knows the very thoughts of our hearts. He knows our doubts when things seem to go all wrong, knows the times when we may even dare to think that we could have planned better than what seems to be God's plan and will for us.

118

How comforting, then, to realize that He understands when our tears fall. I glory in those words in the Revelation, "And God shall wipe away all tears from their eyes" (7:17).

I will always be thankful that when the Lord saw fit to take my beloved husband to be with Him in Glory none of my friends—or *anyone* for that matter—said, "Don't cry, Jeanette." In fact, one close friend came "to cry with me," as she herself explained.

Oh, yes, Jesus cares. He will never be too busy to hear our plea for help. His word is as true for us today as it was when He assured His disciples, "I will not leave you comfortless" (John 14:18). We can confidently put our trust in Him, for He will always be there for us. He *does* care. And—a day at a time—He will meet our deepest needs.

35

THOSE WORDS
WE CAN'T RECALL

Bible Reading: Colossians 3:17-23

Whatsoever ye do, do it heartily (v. 23a).

We can never know when our gracious heavenly Father will take an incident we would rather forget and use it in the life of another Christian.

How well I remember such an instance.

A pastor's wife, I was in our church office where, with a couple of our members, I was folding the church bulletins for the coming Sunday. Noticing that one of the volunteers was not being very particular as to neatness, I chided her, "Will you please be more careful about the corners, Anne?"* to which she responded good-naturedly, "That's just *one*, Mrs. Lockerbie."

"But each person just gets one," I replied, rather smugly, I'm sure. "You wouldn't want that person to judge our church standards by it," and I proceeded to quote to her, "Whatsoever ye do, do it heartily, as to the Lord."

Time went by, time in which I was learning that people's feelings can be more important than a perfectly folded church bulletin. The Lord was teaching me what I should have known long before. But we had moved from that church to another in a different state. And I had no idea where Anne was living.

From time to time I would think of that incident and wish I could recall my smug and unkind words. Then back in the area, one day I was riding the subway, strap-hanging in the crowded car, when at a stop, in came Anne. We instantly recognized each other, and she reached to strap-hang alongside of me. Then she said, "I can't believe it. Just

*Not her real name.

this very morning in my Bible reading I came to a verse that had your initials alongside of it."

Oh, dear Lord, I thought, *What verse would Anne have remembered me by?*

I was not left wondering for long, for above the noise of the train, her face glowing, she said, "Remember that time when you taught me to do things—even seemingly small things—heartily, as to the Lord. I never forgot that lesson." Then, as we left the subway together, she added, "I've often thanked the Lord that you cared enough not to let me do His work in a sloppy fashion."

How good of the Lord to let us have that brief encounter! It brought to mind the lines of a hymn we don't hear much anymore:

> Take all the failures, each mistake
>   Of our poor, foolish ways;
> And, Saviour, for Thine own dear sake
>   Make them show forth Thy praise.

36

LOVING AND LIKING

Bible Reading: John 13:34-35; 15:12

Love one another (13:34b).

Some years ago a missionary guest in our home was effusive over his younger brother, also a missionary. "I love my brother Paul," he commented, adding (and I can still hear him), "Besides that, I *like* the guy."

Loving and liking. Isn't the one inherent in the other?

Before I gave some thought to it, I would have agreed that loving and liking are mutually inclusive. But there appears to be this significant difference: *loving* one another is a matter of obedience to God's command; *liking* is exercising our personal preference and response.

Why might we love, yet not particularly like, an acquaintance?

Generally, if we think it through, we may realize that it is the person's behavior or her attitudes we dislike, not the person herself.

We are all different. We have our quirks and our idiosyncrasies. We develop a certain personality that makes us unique. A few years ago we often heard the phrase "cookie cutter persons," referring to those who were too much alike, in the opinion of other people.

So much for what we *are*, and how it may affect others.

What might be some of the specific reasons we tend not to like or appreciate another person?

Some people alienate others by their talking all the time (I fear I may be one of them).

Another undesirable trait is being a know-it-all. Such persons have the answer to every question, the cure for every ill, the solution to every problem. Still others are chronic gossips, or are argumentative and hard to get along with.

Then there is the negative person who has her list of why it won't work and shouldn't even be attempted; most people are looking for those who will encourage them that "it *will* work."

Nevertheless, we can each learn from the person whose traits we deplore. Nobody's perfect. But, with the help of God, we can begin to both love and like the people with whom we associate daily, thus fulfilling God's command to "love one another."

It's a sobering thought to me as I grow older that someone may be on her knees praying daily for grace to put up with me! To both love me and like me.

37

ONE WAY
TO BECOME POPULAR

Bible Reading: Psalm 81:8-13

Oh, that my people would listen to me! (v. 13a, TLB).

We had just moved to a new church, and, in visiting among the congregation, I was impressed that the mention of a certain woman's name invariably brought warm smiles. Curious, I determined to get to know this woman—and I did. I also observed just how she had created the good feeling that other people had toward her.

Was she especially endowed with abilities that caused her to stand out from the rest of the women in the church?

No, not in specific areas of expertise. But it didn't take long for me to find out where she excelled.

"She *listens*," one after another told me.

Listening: one of the most appreciated traits one can have in a world where, it would seem, nobody wants to listen; everybody wants to talk.

There's a certain selflessness about the woman who will listen to another telling what she wants to tell, even though the matter may not be of particular interest to her.

What does sincere listening say to the one who is talking? It sends the message that what is being said is worth listening to. This can then be easily interpreted by the speaker as, "What I'm saying must be important —and *I* am worth listening to."

There's an art to genuine listening that must not be confused with seeming listening, when the person can hardly wait for the other to stop so that she can have her say.

It takes a heap of patience to be a good listener, especially when the matter is not very interesting, or one is in a hurry.

Is listening, then, an art that we each can cultivate if we care enough to? If we feel that what is being addressed to us is more important at the moment than the thoughts that may be occupying our own mind?

I firmly believe that in most instances it is—and a fringe benefit is that we can become popular, for everyone wants to be listened to.

The word *listen* appears few times in the Bible, but *hear* and *hearken* can be found many times.

Whether we are "hearing" or "hearkening" is immaterial: what is important to good relationships with other people is that we are really *listening*.

38

THE GREATEST GIVING IS FORGIVING

Bible Reading: Ephesians 4:29-32

*Be kind to one another, tenderheart-
ed, forgiving one another (v. 32a,
NKJV).*

A pastor whom I knew very well never
finished a marriage service without exhort-
ing the couple by quoting to them our verse
for today. And how many would greet that
exhortation with looks that said, "Who, *us*,
Pastor? Why would you think *we* will ever
need that verse?" But in the days and years
that followed, more than one couple came
back to thank their pastor for having made

Ephesians 4:32 meaningful in their lives, frequently citing specific occasions.

Not only ministers but the medical profession has in some instances recognized how important a forgiving spirit is for one's well-being. I have a physician friend who has told me, "I could discharge about half of my patients if they could be sure of forgiveness" —obviously the need for it. The lack of it was eating away at their peace of mind. In other cases it was the patient who needed to forgive.

Among the books the Lord has helped me write, I think that the one titled *Forgive: Forget and Be Free* has had the greatest impact on my own life.

How true is the maxim "To err is human, to forgive, divine."

Forgiving is not something that we learn in a day. We can't take a course in it—oh yes, we can! The Bible teaches us specifically the necessity and the value of our having and developing a forgiving spirit.

A thoughtful approach to the subject will cause us to realize that there are three aspects of forgiving:

One: Forgiving the person who has done some wrong toward us.

Two: Being able to forgive ourselves. "If I could only undo that thing, take back those words," and so on.

Three: The most blatant one of all: "I can never forgive *You*, God. You could have prevented (whatever the happening)."

Sometimes we are willing to forgive, but we're miserly with it rather than being generous. "Forgive *as* we are forgiven"— measure for measure. We balance God's scales in our favor when we're generous in forgiving others.

Some of us may forgive, but we don't let ourselves forget. The Indians had a phrase for that: "Burying the hatchet, but keeping the handle sticking up."

And how many times should we be willing to forgive a person?

Matthew records an interesting forgiveness lesson in 18:22, with his account of our Lord's telling Peter to forgive "not seven times but up to seventy times seven." Can

131

you hear Peter say, "But Lord, four hundred and ninety times!" What was Jesus really teaching? I rather think He was saying, "We don't keep score, Peter. We forgive and forgive and forgive." And so He would have us do in our day.

It will cost us to forgive. We may have to humble ourselves, go to the person and seek forgiveness. And not always will we find the other person willing to accept *our* forgiveness. But doing the scriptural thing is its own reward.

In our giving, then, let us not neglect that greatest of all giving: *forgiving*. It can change a life.

39

TURN ANOTHER PAGE

Bible Reading: 1 Samuel 27:1-7

I shall now perish one day at the hand of Saul (v. 1b).

Listen in on the conversation of people, perhaps on the street or in a supermarket. So much of the talk is gloomy predictions or opinions:

"This inflation will kill me."

"Nobody cares one little bit about older folk anymore."

"Our country was never in such bad shape."

You can probably add ten more such dismal statements.

The fact that there may be some truth in the dreary chatter adds no value to it. Such talk just tends to depress the hearers, who are in no position to do anything about the situation. Nevertheless, some of us do fall into the "bad news" trap.

King David himself had fallen into a similar trap, nursing bad news concerning his own welfare rather than conditions in general. Here he was—predicting his own violent death. Worse still, he was talking of seeking refuge with the enemy, the *Philistines!* "Saul's going to kill me," moaned the discouraged David. "I might as well go over to the enemy's side."

How close this is to doubting God and believing the devil. But then Satan is a master at these three D's: *discouragement, doubt,* and *despair.*

Too bad David couldn't turn over a few pages and read of himself as we can: *"And he [David] died in a good old age, full of days, riches, and honor"* (1 Chronicles 29:28).

David had certainly been used badly by King Saul. But he had proved God's power to deliver him—even from a giant!

Does your present set of circumstances seem too much for you to endure?

Do you dread the future?

Do you, perhaps, feel that God has forsaken you?

Does the way of the ungodly sometimes tempt you to forsake your faith?

Running away is never the answer. It wasn't for David; it isn't for you and me. There will be answers as you "turn the page," answers such as these:

"Commit thy way unto the Lord; trust also in him" (Psalm 37:5).

"I am with you always" (Matthew 28:20, NKJV). Hang on to that "always."

"My peace I give unto you" (John 14:27). The peace of *God*.

"I will never leave you nor forsake you" (Hebrews 13:5, NKJV).

May I suggest that, to find your own personal verse from the Lord, you turn the pages of Scripture and—as has so often blessed my heart and soul—let a verse leap from the page as though it was written *just for you*.

135

Your days may be dark, but it's as true today as it was when Hudson Taylor declared it long ago, "The future is as bright as the promises of God."

And who can tell what our good God has in store for you when you turn the next page of your life? Doesn't that excite you?

40

THE LAST RED LETTER VERSE

Bible Reading: Acts 1:1-9

And you shall be witnesses unto Me (v. 8b, NKJV).

Many Bibles have the words of Jesus printed in red letters. Reading in one such Bible a few years ago, I was struck with the significance of the last red letter verse on the page, even more so when I realized that it was the last sentence the Lord Jesus spoke to His disciples before He ascended back to heaven. It was His marching orders to the ones He was counting on to spread the gospel throughout their world: "You shall be witnesses unto me."

Last words have long had special significance. Generally, we go to all lengths to carry out the wishes or commands of a dying loved one. Why, then, I wonder, would we who call ourselves believers in the Lord Jesus Christ, people who love Him, be unheeding or dilatory about His last directive to His followers? Jesus did not say, "You *may* be witnesses." He said, "You *shall*."

Can it be that some of us do not take the word *witness* at its face value? We wrap it in all kinds of trappings until it seems something that only very specially trained persons can do.

What is a witness? It is someone who has firsthand knowledge of the thing in question. Nothing makes for more credibility than being able to say, "I was there. I saw. I know what happened." Such a witness is generally the only evidence permissible in court.

People can pooh-pooh our theories and opinions. They can dispute our reasoning or our argument. But they cannot refute our personal experience. I like the lines of the old hymn:

I was there when it happened,
And I ought to know . . .

Has it ever occurred to you that you have a testimony for Christ that no one else in all the world has? It's yours; it's unique. I love to be in a group when one person starts to share how she came to Christ. Invariably others want to get in on this, and there are as many and as varied accounts as there are people present.

The apostle Paul recognized the inestimable value of a personal testimony. He could have dazzled an audience with his knowledge and varied experiences and eloquence. He could have bragged about his family background every time he had opportunity. He chose not to, opting rather to tell his never-varying account of his life-changing encounter with the living Christ on the Damascus Road.

No one in recorded history had quite the same experience as Paul. But your coming to the Savior—or my coming to know Him —is no less important. And our neighbors and our friends and our yet unsaved loved ones need to know it.

The Lord Jesus Christ is still saying, "You shall be witnesses unto me," and, "Go ye."

It may be that, like many another, you feel that you can best witness through your consistent living. That, too. Nevertheless, we can never discount sharing the Word of God itself, as we seek to win those around us— and it will be a red-letter day for them and for us when we lead them to Christ.

41

WHAT'S HAPPENED TO THE FIFTH COMMANDMENT?

Bible Reading: Exodus 20:3-12

Honour thy father and thy mother (v. 12a).

Struggling to memorize the Ten Commandments for a Sunday school contest, seven-year-old Beth bogged down on the fifth with its "that thy days may be long." Frustrated, she sloughed it off with, "I don't want to be an old lady anyway!"

We can smile at a child's somewhat selfish logic. But as recipients of the grace of God, as professed believers in Him, we cannot so easily dismiss our biblical responsibilities, whatever our age.

What about "Honor thy father and thy mother?"

Much is being said and written these days about the care of the elderly. But what is being done in practical ways to relieve them of their ongoing fears for their future? Such fears as:

- financial problems in a day of rising costs and a fixed income
- fears of sickness with no one to take care of them, in a day when families can be so scattered as to be unavailable to one another
- death robbing them of old friends with whom to fellowship
- changing neighborhoods creating less safe conditions

A more subtle loss, one that becomes gradually apparent, is the loss of self-esteem. It is a loss that comes about when one's ideas and opinions are discounted or pooh-poohed as not being worth considering, thus making the older person shrink from taking part in some conversations.

Listening to, or overhearing, some of these fears expressed, I sense a certain "What-good-am-I-in-the-world-anymore?" despair.

Each of us, whatever our age, needs to remind himself that we are of great worth in the sight of God, that He has plans for each one. Speaking of the righteous, the psalmist writes, "They shall still bring forth fruit in old age" (Psalm 92:14).

Ironically, some countries to which we send missionaries with the gospel message can teach us much about honoring our fathers and our mothers. For example, a woman whom I met on one of my teaching trips to Asian countries confided to me, "My sister, who is much wealthier than I, felt that she should have the pleasure of taking care of our aged mother. But, as the youngest daughter, it is *my privilege.*"

Another instance comes to my mind, this one from Canada, where the grand-mother was so loved and wanted that her grandchildren, not all of whom were Christians, would bribe her to come live with them. She had just a small income and she loved to give to missions, so they would coax,

"Grandma, if you'll come and stay with us, we'll put all our dimes in your missionary bank." That is honoring the fifth commandment!

Circumstances alter cases, and many a willing son or daughter has such a small home that it might not be best for the father or mother to be with them. God knows our heart and our intentions. Where we treat the elderly around us with love and care, it will be counted as our obeying the fifth commandment.

And obedience is its own reward.

The Lord Jesus Himself set the pattern. From the cross, in the midst of His own agony, He remembered His mother and committed her to the care of "the disciple . . . whom he loved" (John 19:26-27).

42

RECLAIMED AND REDEEMED

Bible Reading: 2 Corinthians 5:17-21

All things are become new (v. 17b).

The *Living Bible's* rendition of today's verse is: "When someone becomes a Christian, he [or she] becomes a brand new person inside. He is not the same any more. A new life has begun!"

Who doesn't long for a chance for a new beginning? And all the time, to one who reads and believes the Bible, the opportunity is clearly given.

New eyes to see. New ears to hear what God has done for us. New goals of pleasing Him. New ambitions that go beyond selfish aspirations. Perhaps the most glorious of all the new things in the basket of life after re-demption is our new *destination*: a heaven to look forward to.

Everything new! It's almost too expansive a concept for me. I can get pretty excited over just one new thing: a new book, a new dress. In particular, a new friend or a new idea excites me. And here God is promising us *all* new things. God—who alone can keep every promise He ever makes. No ifs, ands, or buts.

Are you perhaps thinking, *I would settle for a new body, one without any aches or pains?* Fine! That is a part of God's package of new things for every one of us who will let Him reclaim and redeem us. The Bible makes it clear that we will have new bodies, indestructible bodies, a truth tied in with our new destination: The Lord Jesus said, "When everything is ready, then I will come and get you, so that you can always be with me where I am" (John 14:3, TLB).

We're living in a time when recycling is the order of the day. However, any item, no matter how valuable it once was, will remain what it has become—a piece of junk—unless and until it is reclaimed from the trash heap.

There is no hope for it apart from reclamation. It cannot pick itself up. The Bible, always ahead of the times, recognizes the value of recycling human potential.

But first comes the *reclaiming*. David the psalmist knew all about this. He speaks of being in "a horrible pit" and "miry clay" (Psalm 40:2). Doesn't that savor of a garbage pile, a trash heap? But God didn't leave him there. "He brought me up," writes David. Not only that, but God "set [his] feet upon a rock." And as if *that* were not enough, David exults, He "put a new song in [my] mouth."

That is the kind of recycling our God is interested in.

It is our privilege by our life and witness to show others around us how they, too, can be reclaimed and redeemed and made ready for heaven, where all things are new!

43

WHEN WE LOSE A LOVED ONE

Bible Reading: 2 Corinthians 1:1-4

That we may be able to comfort (v. 4b).

I don't really like the expression "losing someone" when we are speaking of one taken in death.

We lose things, but rarely people. But I'll use the well-known phrase for our purposes right now.

What are the real heartaches when our Lord sees fit to take to Himself someone we love and would fain keep with us forever?

Oh, there are always the practical realities that are apparent when the man of the house, the provider and caregiver, is no longer with us.

But, in a truly happy marriage there are other factors. It's the loss of these that can make the day too long, the night seemingly endless, the loss of a good husband the hardest to bear. I speak of a meeting of the minds, a togetherness in which the one can start a sentence and the other finish it. For me it meant my being able to express my ideas—to think out loud with one who was listening and who would help me to hone my thinking, one who would never verbally shoot down an idea. Rather, he would see other facets that might have escaped me. Never was he disinterested in what I was doing.

Adjusting to being deprived of this intimacy of the minds is something that takes time, if indeed we ever do adjust to it.

So, where we can, we do well as fellow Christians to be available to the one who needs to talk out her feelings and know she has a sympathetic listener. This is especially true in the early days of her bereavement when it is all that the grieving person wants to talk about. There's therapy in being allowed to voice—over and over—the feelings of grief.

There are those who have never yet suffered the loss of the one dearest to them on earth. Such persons can't be expected to "comfort one another with the comfort wherewith they themselves have been comforted," to paraphrase Paul. But many will have suffered such loss. For those, a statement made by Billy Graham in his book *Facing Death and the Life Hereafter* rings true: "God does not comfort us to make us comfortable, but to make us comforters."

Undoubtedly, at some point in our lives, we will feel the need to be comforted. May we, then, be willing to pass on that comfort —offer the gift of our time and a listening ear—to someone who needs it.